A Mink, a Fink, a Skating Rink

What Is a Noun?

To Molly, Matt, and Andy—three very proper nouns
                                        —B.P.C.

To my mom, who has always been crazy about cats, and my dad, who surprised me by bringing home a kitten when I was 10
                                        —J.P.

noun: A word that names a person, animal, place, or thing.

A Mink, a Fink, a Skating Rink

What Is a Noun?

by Brian P. Cleary

illustrated by Jenya Prosmitsky

M MILLBROOK PRESS / MINNEAPOLIS

Hill is a noun.
Mill is a noun.

Even uncle Phil is a noun.

In fact, our whole hometown is a noun.

Nouns can sometimes
be quite proper,

Like
Brooklyn Bridge,

or

Edward
Hopper,

A jail,
a nail,
a bale of hay,
The pool or park in
which you play,

A quarter, a porter, a pencil, or pear—

Nouns are seen most everywhere.

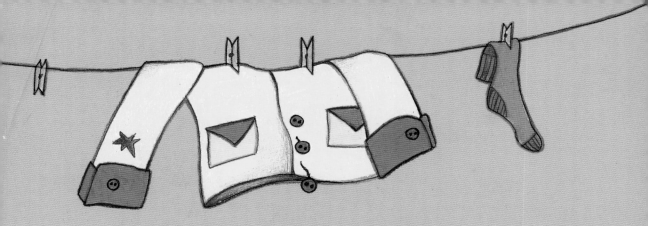

A pocket, button,
sleeve, or cuff—

A noun can simply
be your stuff.

The pope, some soap

that's on a rope,

A downtown mall, a downhill slope.

A
house,
a mouse,
a broken
clock,

WELCOME
TO
SANTA FE

New
Mexico,
an old White
Sock,

Some tar,
a bar,

a baseball star,

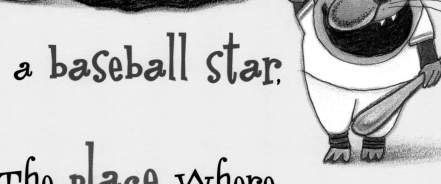

The place where
Mother
parks her
car.

A noun can be your **Auntie Lynn,**

The **mayor** of the **town** you're in,

Your friend
who tells
you corny
jokes—

A noun can be
your favorite folks.

A collar,
a scholar,
a handful
of sand,

Saxes and faxes,
the brass in the band,

A cat, a bat, your grandma's hat—

Nouns are a little of this and that.

If it's a place of any kind—

A mountain, hall, or Highway 9,

If it's a country,
state, or town,

Then surely, shirley,
it's a noun.

A king,
a queen,
some
gasoline,

A red raspberry
ice machine.

ICE

If it's a boat or coat or clown,

It's simple, Simon, it's a noun!

ABOUT THE AUTHOR & ILLUSTRATOR

Brian P. Cleary is the author of the Words Are CATegorical©, Math Is CATegorical©, Food Is CATegorical™, Adventures in Memory™, and Sounds Like Reading™ series. He has also written The Laugh Stand: Adventures in Humor; Peanut Butter and Jellyfishes: A Very Silly Alphabet Book; The Punctuation Station; and two poetry books. Mr. Cleary lives in Cleveland, Ohio.

JENYA PROSMITSKY grew up and studied art in Kishinev, Moldova. Her two cats, Henry and Freddy, were vital to her illustrations for this book.

Copyright © 1999 by Lerner Publishing Group, Inc.

Millbrook Press
A division of Lerner Publishing Group, Inc.
241 First Avenue North
Minneapolis, MN 55401 USA

For reading levels and more information,
look up this title at www.lernerbooks.com.

Library of Congress Cataloging-in-Publication Data

Cleary, Brian P., 1959—
   A mink, a fink, a skating rink : what is a noun? / by Brian P. Cleary ;
illustrated by Jenya Prosmitsky.
     p. cm — (Words are categorical)
   Summary: Rhyming text and illustrations of comical cats present
numerous examples of nouns, from "gown" and "crown" to "boat,"
"coat," and "clown."
   ISBN 978-1-57505-402-5 (lib. bdg. : alk. paper)
   ISBN 978-1-57505-417-9 (pbk. : alk. paper)
   ISBN 978-1-57505-547-3 (EB pdf)
   1. English language—Noun—Juvenile literature. [1. English
language—Noun.] I. Prosmitsky, Jenya, 1974—, ill. II. Title.
III. Series: Cleary, Brian P., 1959— Words are categorical.
PE1201.C58 1999   98—46384
428.2—dc21

Manufactured in China
21-41672-3028-3/23/2016